TUDOR	STUART	GEORGIAN	VICTORIAN	MODERN TIMES
1485–1603	1603–1714	1714–1837	1837–1901	1901–NOW

children's HISTORY of NORWICH

Written by
Peter Kent

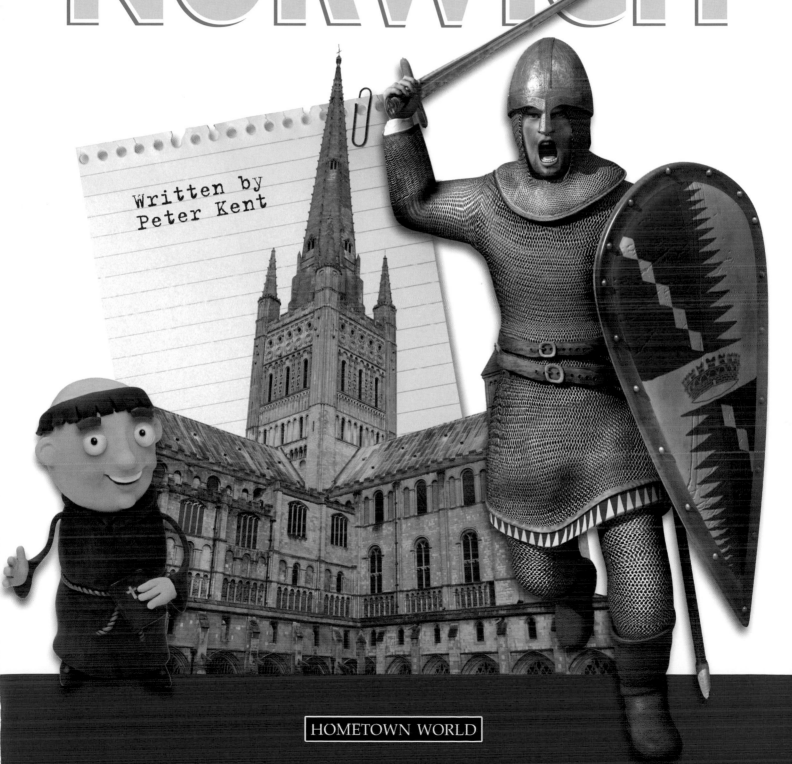

HOMETOWN WORLD

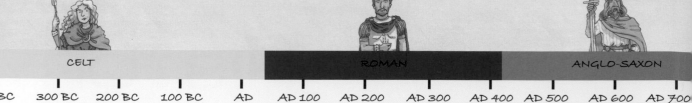

CELT 500 BC · 400 BC · 300 BC · 200 BC · 100 BC · AD · ROMAN AD 100 · AD 200 · AD 300 · AD 400 · ANGLO-SAXON AD 500 · AD 600 · AD 700

How well do you know your town?

Have you ever wondered what it would have been like living in Norwich when the Romans arrived? What about training to be an apprentice for seven years? This book will uncover the important and exciting things that happened in your town.

Want to hear the other good bits? You will love this book! Some rather brainy folk have worked on it to make sure it's fun and informative. So what are you waiting for? Peel back the pages and be amazed at what happened in your town.

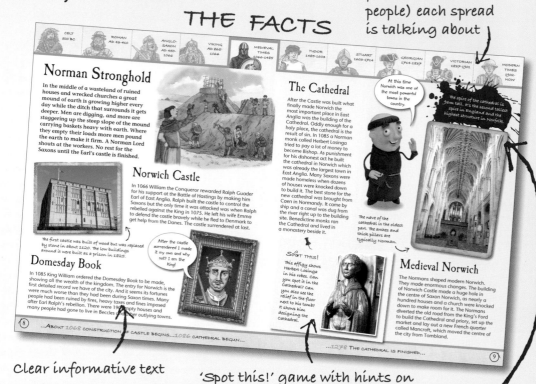

Timeline shows which period (dates and people) each spread is talking about

Clear informative text

'Spot this!' game with hints on something to find in your town

Hometown facts to amaze you!

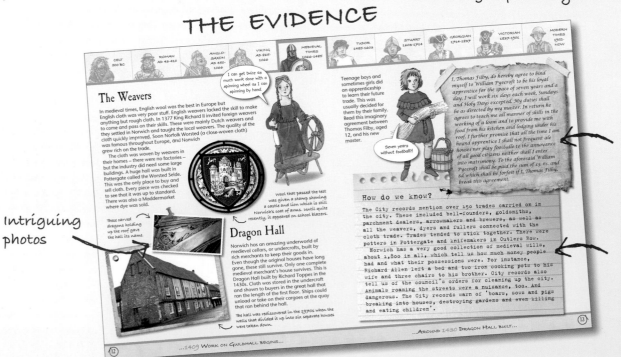

Go back in time to read what it was like for children growing up in Norwich

Intriguing photos

Each period in the book ends with a summary explaining how we know about the past

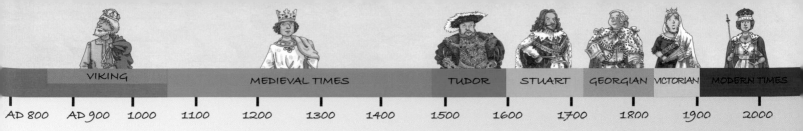

Contents

CELT
500 BC

ROMAN
AD 43-410

ANGLO-SAXON
AD 450-1066

VIKING
AD 865-1066

MEDIEVAL TIMES
1066-1485

The Roman Town

It was rough crossing the North Sea and Livia wondered if they'd ever reach the estuary of the River Yare safely. It took a day to sail through the mud banks and marshes, before turning into the smaller River Tas. Finally, in the evening light, their ship reached the town of Venta Icenorum. Livia has come with her parents for her father's work. Navius is a lawyer and will work in the basilica (law courts). Venta Icenorum is about as far away from Rome as you can get but they will be comfortable. Livia's villa is one of the largest and most luxurious villas in Venta Icenorum. She can't wait to explore her new home!

Yes, this will do nicely.

SPOT THIS!

Can you spot the Roman brick that was brought to Norwich and reused in the Cathedral? It's nearly twice as old as the cathedral!

Boudicca's Revolt

There was no town where Norwich stands when the Romans invaded Britain in AD 43 although there were farms and settlements inhabited by a powerful tribe called the Iceni. The Iceni did not fight the Romans and for a few years all was peaceful. Then, in AD 60, the king of the Iceni died and the Romans seized all his treasure and brutally treated his daughters and widow, Boudicca. She gathered her tribe and attacked the Romans with help from their neighbours, the Trinovantes. The Iceni destroyed the new Roman colony of Colchester and burnt London and Verulamium (near St Albans). It looked as if the Romans would be driven out of Britain but a legion hurried back from fighting in Wales to defeat the rebels. Boudicca poisoned herself to avoid capture.

I shall have revenge on the Romans. Go home to Rome!

AD 43 ROMANS ARRIVE IN BRITAIN...AD 70 VENTA ICENORUM IS FOUNDED...

TUDOR
1485-1603

STUART
1603-1714

GEORGIAN
1714-1837

VICTORIAN
1837-1901

MODERN
TIMES
1902-NOW

The New Town

After the revolt of Boudicca the Romans set up a new capital for the Iceni near modern Norwich in what is now called Caistor St Edmunds. They chose a site with good river and road connections surrounded by fertile farm lands. They called it Venta Icenorum or the Market of the Iceni. The local government officials and those Iceni who wanted to live like Romans lived there. It was soon a bustling town with a market and workshops making glass, bronze brooches and pottery.

Ships brought luxury goods and wine to the town and returned full of corn. There were three temples, a forum and public baths as well as houses that seemed like palaces compared with the huts of the Iceni. There was even a small amphitheatre. In about AD 280 the fear of barbarian raids made the citizens build a defensive wall with towers and four gates.

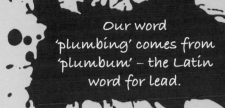
Our word 'plumbing' comes from 'plumbum' – the Latin word for lead.

This is a painting of what Venta Icenorum may have looked like.

How do we know?

Inside the old walls today there is just a field with nothing to see. Nobody knew that there was anything worth looking for until a pilot flying overhead in 1928 saw regular patterns in the grass. It was a very dry summer and the grass over old roads and buildings grew less than the rest of the field. The pilot saw and photographed the regular grid of a Roman street plan. This showed archaeologists where to dig and they uncovered the gates, forum, baths and several houses of Venta Icenorum. Amongst their finds were many brooches, tiny babies' bracelets and part of a blue glass cup showing a chariot race. The cockle shells found all over the site tell us just how much the Romans loved their seafood.

The Romans were ordered to leave Britain in AD 410 to try to save Rome from invaders.

... ABOUT AD 450 THE TOWN IS ABANDONED...

CELT
500 BC

ROMAN
AD 43-410

ANGLO-SAXON
AD 450-1066

VIKING
AD 865-1066

MEDIEVAL TIMES
1066-1485

The Anglo-Saxon Chronicle

In this year, 1004, the terrible Sweyn Forkbeard, King of Denmark, came with all his fleet of longships, each full of warriors, merciless and greedy for plunder. He sailed up the river to Norwic and many of the townsfolk fled at his coming. The cruel Vikings set people's homes on fire. None were spared: the old, the weak, women and infants, all fell to the fury of the Norsemen. When Sweyn sailed back to the sea, his ships sat low in the water with all their loot and nothing was left of Norwic except ashes.

Run for your lives!

This carving on Saint Lawrence's doorway shows King Edmund, being used as target practice by the Vikings. There is a wolf poking out of the bushes. It guarded the King's body until it was taken away to be buried.

Saxons Settle

The history of Norwich itself really begins after the Romans left in AD 410. The Saxons, who had been raiding from across the North Sea, came to settle. They drove the Britons into the west and set up seven separate kingdoms. East Anglia was one of them. In about AD 600 the Saxons began to settle in the river valley where Norwich is now. They had no use for the old town of Venta and it soon fell into ruin. In the Middle Ages the stone and bricks were carted off to build Norwich. In AD 869 the Saxons were attacked by Vikings from Scandinavia. Vikings killed Edmund, the last King of East Anglia, and many more Danes came to settle. Fifty years later the Saxon and Danish lands were united in one Kingdom of England. The Vikings attacked again in AD 991 and kept coming back. In 1004, King Sweyn of Denmark destroyed Norwich, which by then had grown into an important town.

...ABOUT AD 600 SAXONS BEGIN TO SETTLE...AD 869 KING EDMUND KILLED...

Four into One

Fifteen hundred years ago there was nothing where Norwich stands today except the crossing of two Roman roads and their fords across the River Wensum. This spot attracted Saxon settlers and, after a while, four small and separate villages developed. Coslany (which means piggies long island) and Northwic were to the north of the river. Connesford (The King's Ford) was where the Cathedral now stands and Westwic about a kilometre to the west. There may have been a fifth hamlet called Needham but, if so, it was very small and poor. The Saxons then ruled until 1066 when Harold was beaten by William the Conqueror at the Battle of Hastings and the history of Anglo-Saxon England ended as the Norman invaders took control.

SPOT THIS!

Can you spot the street names, Colegate, Cowgate and Fishergate? The Danish ending for street was gat.

A hoard of about 33 Anglo-Saxon items was found at Harford Farm near Norwich. This brooch was one of the items covered with gold leaf and set with garnets. Other items found were three gold pendants, two silver coins and a belt buckle.

Between the 8th and 11th centuries the Vikings took over most of northern Europe.

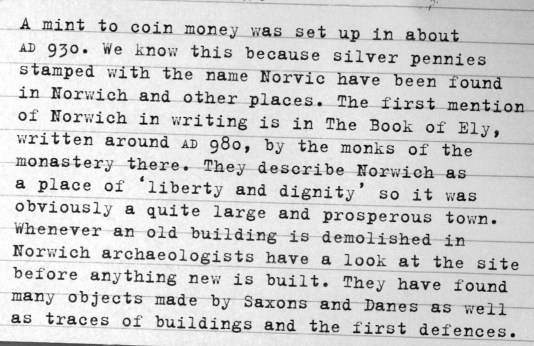

How do we know?

A mint to coin money was set up in about AD 930. We know this because silver pennies stamped with the name Norvic have been found in Norwich and other places. The first mention of Norwich in writing is in The Book of Ely, written around AD 980, by the monks of the monastery there. They describe Norwich as a place of 'liberty and dignity' so it was obviously a quite large and prosperous town. Whenever an old building is demolished in Norwich archaeologists have a look at the site before anything new is built. They have found many objects made by Saxons and Danes as well as traces of buildings and the first defences.

CELT
500 BC

ROMAN
AD 43-410

ANGLO-
SAXON
AD 450-
1066

VIKING
AD 865-
1066

MEDIEVAL
TIMES
1066-1485

Norman Stronghold

In the middle of a wasteland of ruined houses and wrecked churches a great mound of earth is growing higher every day while the ditch that surrounds it gets deeper. Men are digging, and more are staggering up the steep slope of the mound carrying baskets heavy with earth. Where they empty their loads more men pound the earth to make it firm. A Norman Lord shouts at the workers. No rest for the Saxons until the Earl's castle is finished.

Norwich Castle

In 1066 William the Conqueror rewarded Ralph Guader for his support at the Battle of Hastings by making him Earl of East Anglia. Ralph built the castle to control the Saxons but the only time it was attacked was when Ralph rebelled against the King in 1075. He left his wife Emma to defend the castle bravely while he fled to Denmark to get help from the Danes. The castle surrendered at last.

The first castle was built of wood but was replaced by stone in about 1120. The low buildings around it were built as a prison in 1825.

After the castle surrendered I made it my own and why not? I am the King!

Domesday Book

In 1085 King William ordered the Domesday Book to be made, showing all the wealth of the kingdom. The entry for Norwich is the first detailed record we have of the city. And it seems its fortunes were much worse than they had been during Saxon times. Many people had been ruined by fires, heavy taxes and fines imposed after Earl Ralph's rebellion. There were 190 empty houses and many people had gone to live in Beccles and other outlying towns.

...ABOUT 1068 CONSTRUCTION OF CASTLE BEGINS...1086 CATHEDRAL BEGUN...

TUDOR
1485-1603

STUART
1603-1714

GEORGIAN
1714-1837

VICTORIAN
1837-1901

MODERN
TIMES
1902-
NOW

The Cathedral

After the Castle was built what finally made Norwich the most important place in East Anglia was the building of the cathedral. Oddly enough for a holy place, the cathedral is the result of sin. In 1085 a Norman monk called Herbert Losinga tried to pay a lot of money to become Bishop. As punishment for his dishonest act he built the cathedral in Norwich which was already the largest town in East Anglia. Many Saxons were made homeless when dozens of houses were knocked down to build it. The best stone for the new cathedral was brought from Caen in Normandy. It came by ship and a canal was dug from the river right up to the building site. Benedictine monks ran the cathedral and lived in a monastery beside it.

At this time Norwich was one of the most powerful towns in the country.

The spire of the cathedral is 96m tall. It's the second tallest spire in England and the highest structure in Norfolk.

The nave of the cathedral is the oldest part. The arches and thick pillars are typically Norman.

SPOT THIS!

This effigy shows Herbert Losinga in his robes. Can you spot it in the Cathedral? Can you also see the relief in the floor next to his tomb? It shows him designing the Cathedral.

Medieval Norwich

The Normans shaped modern Norwich. They made enormous changes. The building of Norwich Castle made a huge hole in the centre of Saxon Norwich, as nearly a hundred houses and a church were knocked down to make room for it. The Normans diverted the old road from the King's Ford to build the cathedral and priory, set up the market and lay out a new French quarter called Mancroft, which moved the centre of the city from Tombland.

CELT
500 BC

ROMAN
AD 43-410

ANGLO-
SAXON
AD 450-
1066

VIKING
AD 865-
1066

MEDIEVAL
TIMES
1066-1485

Norwich Becomes a City

King Richard the Lionheart first made Norwich a city in 1109. By 1400 Norwich was the second richest city in England and its wealth bought a charter from King Henry IV in 1404. This made Norwich a county, like Norfolk or Yorkshire, with complete self-government. No one outside the city, except the King, had any power there. The ruling council was run by rich merchants. The city decided it needed something very grand to house its new council and began building the Guildhall in 1407. It was also used as a law court, with a prison in the basement and an armoury to keep the city's guns.

A law forced citizens to work on the Guildhall from 5 o'clock in the morning to 8 o'clock at night as often as they were needed.

Hospitals

The hospitals weren't like those today where the sick are cured but more like care homes for the poor and old. The Great Hospital in Bishopgate was set up by Bishop Suffield in 1249 for the care of 'old and decayed' priests but it also had beds for 30 poor patients. Saint Paul's Hospital was the only one to care for pregnant women. Most people had to rely on their relatives to look after them. When the Black Death arrived in the city, about one in three people – about 8,000 – died.

Norwich had six leper hospitals outside the city walls, as lepers weren't allowed in through the gates.

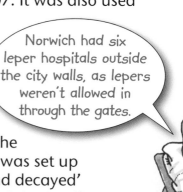

The Walled City

Most medieval cities had walls, not so much to defend them against invading armies but as a way of controlling who went in and out. Norwich was first surrounded by a bank and ditch but in 1297 a stone wall was begun, although it wasn't finished until 1344. It was built of flint. There were 12 gates and over 40 towers. To the east there were no walls, as the river acted as a moat. The area enclosed by the walls was bigger than London but, as Norwich had only a tenth of London's population, there was plenty of room and it was famous as a city of gardens. The river was guarded by two towers. The unwalled stretch by the Cathedral was guarded by the Cow Tower.

Ethelbert Gate was one of two main gates leading into Norwich Cathedral precinct.

...1344 WALLS FINISHED...1349 BLACK DEATH IN THE CITY...

TUDOR
1485-1603

STUART
1603-1714

GEORGIAN
1714-1837

VICTORIAN
1837-1901

MODERN
TIMES
1902-
NOW

Peasant's Revolt

In 1381, a peasant army led a revolt against the ruling class. It started in South Essex and travelled to Norwich. The peasants wanted all men below the king to be treated as equal. Richard II had introduced a poll tax of 5p for every tax payer, on top of other poll taxes which had already been introduced. This was a lot of money to the poor and left them even poorer. People were also angry over the attempt to reduce wages back to what they had been before the Black Death. The divide between rich and poor became huge. The rebel army set fire to the houses of wealthy citizens and lawyers in Norwich.

The walls of Norwich could not protect it from the Peasant's Revolt. Nothing could. People were fighting for their rights.

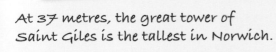
At 37 metres, the great tower of Saint Giles is the tallest in Norwich.

A City of Churches

A lot of the wealth of the city went into building or rebuilding churches. When people died they usually left some money to their local parish church. If they were very rich they had a chapel built with a priest to say prayers for their soul. As well as the cathedral and its priory of monks, there were four friaries, an abbey of nuns and fifty-seven churches. Even in medieval times it was far too many.

If every single person in Norwich had gone to church at the same time there would still have been plenty of room to spare.

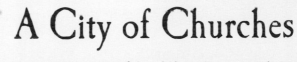
The Cow Tower, built in 1380, is one of the earliest brick buildings in England. It cost the city about £36.77 to build.

CELT
500 BC

ROMAN
AD 43-410

ANGLO-
SAXON
AD 450-
1066

VIKING
AD 865-
1066

MEDIEVAL
TIMES
1066-1485

I can get twice as much work done with a spinning wheel as I can spinning by hand.

The Weavers

In medieval times, English wool was the best in Europe but English cloth was very poor stuff. English weavers lacked the skill to make anything but rough cloth. In 1377 King Richard II invited foreign weavers to come and pass on their skills. These were mainly Dutch weavers and they settled in Norwich and taught the local weavers. The quality of the cloth quickly improved. Soon Norfolk Worsted (a close-woven cloth) was famous throughout Europe, and Norwich grew rich on the trade.

The cloth was woven by weavers in their homes – there were no factories – but the industry did need some large buildings. A huge hall was built in Pottergate called the Worsted Selde. This was the only place to buy and sell cloth. Every piece was checked to see that it was up to standard. There was also a Maddermarket where dye was sold.

Wool that passed the test was given a stamp showing a castle and lion which is still Norwich's coat of arms. Until quite recently, it appeared on school blazers.

These carved dragons holding up the roof gave the hall its name.

Dragon Hall

Norwich has an amazing underworld of medieval cellars, or undercrofts, built by rich merchants to keep their goods in. Even though the original houses have long gone, these still survive. Only one complete medieval merchant's house survives. This is Dragon Hall built by Richard Toppes in the 1430s. Cloth was stored in the undercroft and shown to buyers in the great hall that ran the length of the first floor. Ships could unload or take on their cargoes at the quay that ran behind the hall.

The hall was rediscovered in the 1970s when the walls that divided it up into six separate houses were taken down.

...1409 WORK ON GUILDHALL BEGINS...

Teenage boys and sometimes girls did an apprenticeship to learn their future trade. This was usually decided for them by their family. Read this imaginary agreement between Thomas Filby, aged 12, and his new master.

Seven years without football?!

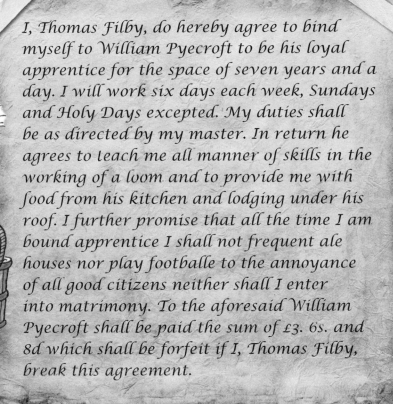

I, Thomas Filby, do hereby agree to bind myself to William Pyecroft to be his loyal apprentice for the space of seven years and a day. I will work six days each week, Sundays and Holy Days excepted. My duties shall be as directed by my master. In return he agrees to teach me all manner of skills in the working of a loom and to provide me with food from his kitchen and lodging under his roof. I further promise that all the time I am bound apprentice I shall not frequent ale houses nor play footballe to the annoyance of all good citizens neither shall I enter into matrimony. To the aforesaid William Pyecroft shall be paid the sum of £3. 6s. and 8d which shall be forfeit if I, Thomas Filby, break this agreement.

How do we know?

The city records mention over 150 trades carried on in the city. These included bell-founders, goldsmiths, parchment dealers, arrowmakers and brewers, as well as all the weavers, dyers and fullers connected with the cloth trade. Trades tended to stick together. There were potters in Pottergate and knifemakers in Cutlers Row.

Norwich has a very good collection of medieval wills, about 1,800 in all, which tell us how much money people had and what their possessions were. For instance, Richard Allen left a bed and two iron cooking pots to his wife and three chairs to his brother. City records also tell us of the council's orders for cleaning up the city. Animals roaming the streets were a nuisance, too. And dangerous. The city records warn of 'boars, sows and pigs breaking into houses, destroying gardens and even killing and eating children'.

CELT
500 BC

ROMAN
AD 43-410

ANGLO-
SAXON
AD 450-
1066

VIKING
AD 865-
1066

MEDIEVAL
TIMES
1066-
1485

Under Siege

As night falls over the frightened city the bright fires of the rebel camp burn like stars on the heights above. In his house before the Cathedral gate Augustine Steward, the Lord Mayor, anxiously checks that the servants have fitted extra bolts to the doors. It's been a long and frightening day with the guns booming from Mousehold and cannon balls felling chimneys and smashing roofs. Tomorrow the rebels will surely attack. Will the gates and walls hold? Will every citizen be loyal? Somewhere, a musket shot cracks and a dozen dogs begin to bark.

The Cow Tower was badly damaged by the rebels' guns. You can still see the damage.

Forty-nine rebels were hanged. So great was the strain that the gallows broke.

Kett's Rebellion

In the late 1540s, the country was suffering from higher food prices and rent. Things got worse when the rich began to fence off land for their sheep to graze on. This land had been shared by the rich and poor for centuries. Now the poor became poorer as they could no longer farm.

In 1549, no longer able to watch the rich get richer, the poor began to tear down the fences. Robert Kett, a local landowner, joined the rebel army before they could attack him. He led about 10,000 men to Norwich and camped on Mousehold Heath. The rebel army got bigger and they began attacking the city. Cannon balls were fired and they bombarded the walls and captured the city. The rebels were defeated and Robert Kett was hanged from the castle as a terrible warning.

Hard Times

The 1500s were a time of great change in Norwich. When Henry VIII closed the monasteries, the monks left the cathedral and the great church of the Black Friars was closed and turned into a public hall. Kett's rebellion caused a lot of damage and the wool trade began to lose money. The Norwich weavers were making old fashioned heavy cloths which didn't sell well. Trade was so bad that grass grew in the market place.

In 1565, the Mayor invited 30 families of refugees from Flanders to come and work and teach new ways of weaving. Some spoke Dutch, others French and they were given two churches of their own. They became known as the 'strangers'.

Hmmm, he's got a funny accent.

Quiet at the back. I am here to teach you, so pay attention!

As well as their textile skills, the strangers brought their hobby of breeding pet canaries, for which Norwich soon became famous. Norwich City Football Club adopted the canary as its badge and nickname.

The New Draperies

The strangers' secret was not in weaving cloth but in finishing it. They could treat ordinary wool cloth so that it had a silky feel and a shimmering surface. They could also dye cloth in many colours. This material was much lighter, and was used for shawls, scarves and fashionable dresses.

The 'strangers' from Flanders helped make Norwich prosperous again.

SPOT THIS!

This plaque is set in a wall near the Cathedral. It marks the spot where Lord Sheffield was dragged from his horse and killed by Fulke the carpenter in the battle of Kett's Rebellion.

NEAR THIS PLACE WAS KILLED LORD SHEFFIELD IN KETT'S REBELLION 1st AUGUST 1549.

Verily but this childe is a marvel. A prodigie of learning!

Royal Visit

Queen Elizabeth I made her only visit to Norwich in August 1578. She stayed nearly a week. There was a continual round of feasting and entertainments. All the Lords from Norfolk came to pay their respects and give her presents. When she left, the Lord Mayor presented her with a purse of gold and she knighted him saying, 'I have laid up in my breast such good will as I shall never forget Norwich.'

Trusty and right well beloved cousin

This day Her great and Glorious Majestie, Our beloved Queen Elizabeth did grace our citie with her presence. I was up before dawn to gain a good place to spy her entrance through St Stephen's Gate but so, it seemeth, was every Tom, Dick and Harry. But, being small and with sharp elbows, I did wriggle through. About three hours I waited thus and would have fainted but for the pedlars who sold bread and sweetmeats. There was a fountain playing, with wine and beer.

At about 9 o'clock in the morning, the Queen and all her train arrived. They say there were over 600 riding behind her and even the meanest servant was arrayed like a lord. The Queen did ride through the gate on a white horse and she waved most friendly and gracious. She looketh very like the portrait the Mayor hath in the Guildhall but not quite so comely. Her skin is very white but I suspect some art hath played its part in that and her teeth, when she smileth, are as stumpy and black as old Mother Hubbard's. The Lord Mayor greeted her kneeling in the road and then

Her Majestie listened to a speech all in Latin said by a boy from the Grammar school dressed as an angel. Her Majestie seemed very pleased at this and said it was right prettily done.

Setting the Record Straight: Three Wrong facts about the Queen's visit.

1 Elizabeth did not sleep in the Maid's Head Hotel.

2 There was no banquet for her in the cathedral cloisters.

3 She did not bring the plague to Norwich. That arrived a month later.

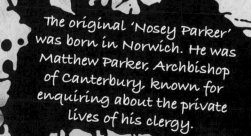
The original 'Nosey Parker' was born in Norwich. He was Matthew Parker, Archbishop of Canterbury, known for enquiring about the private lives of his clergy.

Two Famous Visitors

Will Kemp was an actor and friend of Shakespeare. In 1599, he made a bet that he could morris dance all the way from London to Norwich. He set out with his drummer, and four weeks later he was in Norwich. When he arrived, huge crowds had gathered to watch him finish. He finished his epic dance by Saint John Maddermarket, and with a final roll of the drum, leapt right over the wall into the churchyard.

The actual dancing took only nine days but he took long rests along the way.

This painting from 1568 shows the impressive Cathedral and walls surrounding Norwich.

How do we know?

Bernard Garter wrote an account of Elizabeth's visit to Norwich which includes all the speeches made in Latin to the Queen by the Lord Mayor, Robert Wood. It was a good job Elizabeth could read, write and speak Latin, otherwise she might have been very bored.

Just outside the city over the river beyond Bishop's Bridge was a disused chalk pit where heretics and those who questioned the teachings of the Roman Catholic Church were burned to death. (There's a DIY store on the spot today.)

During the reign of Queen Mary, who was a particularly keen Catholic, 48 people died in what was known as the Lollards' Pit. A brave young woman called Cicely Pine who went to comfort two victims as they were chained to the stake, was arrested, questioned about her religious beliefs and was also burned to death.

This print shows a victim being burned at the stake for heresy at Lollard's Pit.

CELT
500 BC

ROMAN
AD 43-410

ANGLO-
SAXON
AD 450-
1066

VIKING
AD 865-
1066

MEDIEVAL
TIMES
1066-
1485

Trouble and Strife

'Oh Lord what wicked work was here! The soldiers bashed down the door then got to work shattering the stained glass! They beat down statues! Tore up monuments! They pulled down seats! Even pulling out brass from the graves and defacing pictures! The organ pipes were destroyed. The cathedral filled with rude and nasty musketeers. And then what a hideous triumph on market day, when all the ceremonial robes and gowns with all the service and singing books were set on fire in the market place.'

Norwich had the first public library in England. It opened in 1608.

> I don't know how I'll get an education now the Puritans have abolished the choir.

Norwich versus the King

When the Civil War began in 1642, Norwich was against the King and for Parliament. The walls were repaired and cannon mounted on the castle mound. Royalists were persecuted and even the Bishop was forced out of his palace. Many of the soldiers were puritans who wanted all churches to be plain and simple. They smashed up the cathedral, eager to destroy all its decorations and would have demolished it altogether if they could have.

Many men volunteered for the Roundhead army, and the girls of Norwich raised enough money to equip a unit of cavalry who were known as 'The Maiden's Troop'. (Not as menacing as 'Cromwell's Ironsides'!)

SPOT THIS!

Can you spot this statue of Sir Thomas Browne? He was knighted by the King and was Norwich's most famous citizen of the time, a famous scientist and doctor.

TUDOR
1485-1603

STUART
1603-1714

GEORGIAN
1714-1837

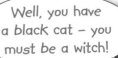

VICTORIAN
1837-1901

MODERN
TIMES
1902-NOW

Witches and Bottles

During the Civil War one man brought great fear to the people of Norwich and East Anglia. General Matthew Hopkins came to Norwich in 1645. He led witch-hunts and was paid by the local magistrate for every witch found guilty. There was a strong belief in witches, magic and the works of the devil. If a woman had a slight imperfection on her skin such as a funny birthmark, or a boil, or perhaps if she lived alone, she might be suspected of being a witch. She would then be brought to trial and if found guilty, would be hanged. Matthew Hopkins tried 40 supposed witches and executed 20. Many houses had a witch bottle buried under the threshold. This contained the owner's urine, locks of hair, pins and charms written on paper, and was supposed to ward off witch's curses.

Well, you have a black cat – you must be a witch!

Read the imaginary account of 12-year old Patience Thurgood who watched the excitement from her gable window.

The Great Blow

The only fighting that took place in Norwich during the Civil War was nothing more than a riot. In 1648 Parliament summoned the mayor, John Utting, to London as a suspected royalist. A crowd of 2,000 demonstrated, then stormed the Committee House, the headquarters of the Roundheads, after a boy was shot. The house, which stood opposite the modern fire station, was full of weapons and barrels of gunpowder. The rioters broke in and began looting and then there was a huge explosion. The Committee House was blown to pieces, all the windows of St Peter Mancroft and St Stephen's were shattered and 40 people were killed. The next day, John Utting rode to London to avoid causing further trouble.

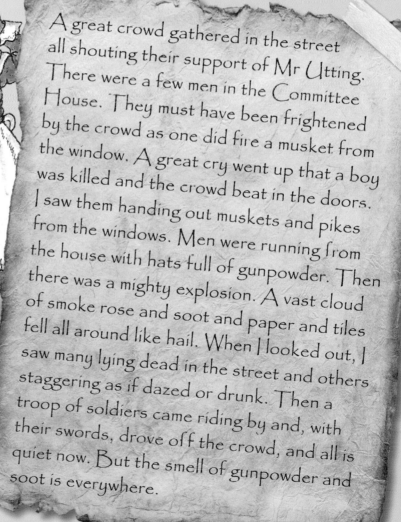

A great crowd gathered in the street all shouting their support of Mr Utting. There were a few men in the Committee House. They must have been frightened by the crowd as one did fire a musket from the window. A great cry went up that a boy was killed and the crowd beat in the doors. I saw them handing out muskets and pikes from the windows. Men were running from the house with hats full of gunpowder. Then there was a mighty explosion. A vast cloud of smoke rose and soot and paper and tiles fell all around like hail. When I looked out, I saw many lying dead in the street and others staggering as if dazed or drunk. Then a troop of soldiers came riding by and, with their swords, drove off the crowd, and all is quiet now. But the smell of gunpowder and soot is everywhere.

A Riotous Time!

The castle ditches are filled with a mob of shrieking, yelling people. A whole army banging drums and washboards and blowing trumpets. The poor preacher is surrounded by 50 or so of his friends beating back the mob with their hymn books. But it's no good. He can't be heard above the din and a continual shower of mud and muck splatters him with filth. There goes his hat! And his wig! His bald head runs with blood and his clothes are torn to tatters. At last he manages to escape to the Griffin Inn. Will the doors hold until the mayor and constables come to rescue him?

The Octagon Chapel is still used today as a place of worship. It was nicknamed 'The Devil's Cucumber Frame.'

Georgian Times

The main industry of Norwich was still making cloth, which was sent all over the world, but brewing beer and making shoes were also becoming important industries, which attracted the wealthy and business. In the 1790s, two large Norwich Union insurance societies were founded, now called Aviva. But the insurance companies weren't like ours today. The Fire Office had its own fire brigade and engines and would only put out a fire in a house if it was insured with the company.

Although most of the houses in the city were still Tudor or medieval, the Georgians added some fine buildings. Many were designed by Thomas Ivory and included The Assembly House, where the gentry gathered for entertainment, Churchman House, built for a rich merchant, and the wonderful Octagon Chapel.

You can still see the fire markers around Norwich.

...1720 RIOTS...1754 OCTAGON CHAPEL BUILT...1760 MORE RIOTS...

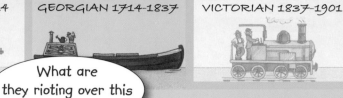

What are they rioting over this time?!

Rioting Norwich

Despite its many churches and tranquil gardens, Norwich was famous for its riots in the 18th century. The citizens rioted over a dozen times: to stop Methodists preaching, on the choice of Mayor, on the shortage of grain, on the lack of jobs and in sympathy with the French Revolution. Sometimes soldiers had to be sent but usually the Mayor managed to restore order.

Davey Place runs between Market Place and Castle Meadow.

The King's Head

One day, in a remarkable publicity stunt, John Davey announced in the Guildhall, 'Gentleman, I mean to put a hole in the King's Head.' He refused to explain what he meant and his house was guarded and the road to London patrolled in case he set off to kill George III. A week later Davey bought the King's Head Inn on the Market place and demolished it to build Norwich's first pedestrian shopping street, Davey Place.

Norwich is famous for having the first modern pedestrianised street in Britain (London Street in 1968.)

The Poor

In the 18th century, there were no benefits paid to poor people in their own homes. They had to go and live in the workhouse, where life was deliberately made hard: both to save money and to discourage people from asking for relief. Norwich had two workhouses: one was in part of the Duke of Norfolk's Palace in Duke Street and the other in what is now the Bridewell Museum. In the winter there were usually about 1,200 people in both houses. Conditions were so bad that people committed suicide and a boy was killed trying to escape through the privy.

How do we know?

The workhouse books tell much about the lives of poor people. Inquests on how people died are useful sources too, especially about the dangers at work. In 1820, Stephen Sutton was working on his master's windmill when he was hit on the head by the sail and died.

The Railway Arrives

No one gets too close to the tall funnelled locomotive standing, hissing gently at the head of the train. Why, it might explode! A crowd of gentlemen and ladies in their best clothes are getting into the carriages. Some cast worried looks at the tall chimney of the engine. Will the sparks set their dresses on fire? With a toot of its whistle and a gale of cheering the train sets off with a jerk – the engine driver hasn't had much practice – and a brass band in the first carriage begins to play 'Hail the Conquering Hero comes'.

Goodness me, it sounds like a monster!

SPOT THIS!

The Victorians started the movement of kindness to animals. This drinking trough was provided for cab horses by a charity. Can you spot it in Castle Meadow?

At one time, there were three stations in Norwich. Thorpe Station is now known as Norwich Station.

Linking Towns

Norwich's first railway opened in 1844, linking the city to Yarmouth from a station by the river at Thorpe. The engineer was the famous George Stephenson. The next year, another railway linked Norwich to Cambridge and London and, the year after that, another line opened to London via Ipswich. Travel was now cheaper and faster. People could go for a day out at the seaside at Yarmouth. A lot of the passengers were four-footed. Huge numbers of cattle arrived at Trowse Station and were driven into the city to be sold in the cattle market. By the end of the 1800s, Norwich had three railway stations.

Hang on. If we're delivering shoes, why aren't we wearing any?!

Boot and Shoe

The cloth industry withered away in the 1800s because Norwich had no cheap source of power, unlike the water and steam-powered mills of the north. And when cheap coal arrived by train it was too late. But the shoe industry grew to replace it. At first, the shoes were all hand made. One person, a clicker, would cut the leather, the cordwainer would make the sole and the finisher would stitch it all together. They all worked at home or in small workshops and the streets were full of children running from place to place with bundles of half-finished shoes. By 1900, big factories were built, with sewing machinery, which replaced the homeworkers.

Keen as Mustard

In 1856, Jeremiah Colman moved from his mill at Stoke Holy Cross just outside Norwich and set up his works making mustard at Carrow Road. Soon Colman's Mustard was famous throughout the world and the works grew and grew. By 1890 Colman made starch, flour and washing powder as well and had over 3,000 workers.

The packaging hasn't changed much over the years.

Jeremiah Colman was a very good employer and built houses for the workers and a school, and provided a nurse and canteen.

Civic Pride

Although Norwich was still basically a medieval city in the 1800s, changes were happening. The streets were paved and lit by gas. The city spread beyond the walls and a brand new street was built to connect Thorpe Station with the centre. A barracks was built on Mousehold Heath and the Castle was converted from a prison to a museum and art gallery. While it was still a prison the last public hanging in England took place outside in 1867. It was such an entertainment that special trains brought spectators from all over Norfolk and Suffolk.

By the 1890s there was a network of railways all over Norfolk, all leading to Norwich. Nowhere in the county was more than 10 kilometres away from a railway station. It was much easier now for country people to get to the city. Here's a letter to her parents from 11-year-old Edith, who has gone to Norwich for the day to see her sister Mabel, who is working as a maid in a big house.

It's nigh on thirty years since you was last up the city and I bet you wouldn't recognise the place! Mabel says it's progress. The cathedral's still there and the castle but there's grand new buildings and a whole new street running down to the station full of shops with huge glass windows. They've got one of those new places that make electric light. They lit up the market place for the Queen's Jubilee and the old folk said the light were so bright it hurt their eyes. And they're widening the streets and laying tracks for them new trams. I can't wait to come back next year and ride on one. Opposite the old market there's a beautiful arcade with all the shops under a glass roof. It's made of shiny tiles, coloured like peacocks, and Mabel says it's as if a piece of the Arabian nights has been dropped into the heart of the old city.

The colourful glazed tiles were made by the famous Dalton firm in Bristol.

New Buildings

The man who did most to change the face of Norwich was architect George Skipper who, with his great rival Edward Boardman, built most of the big new buildings in Norwich from 1890 onwards. Skipper's biggest and most important building is the Norwich Union head office. The colourful Royal Arcade is his best-known and best-loved building.

Skipper had this frieze made for the front of his office, which is now part of Jarrold's department store. It shows him giving orders to builders, accompanied by his daughter and his dog.

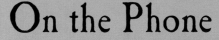

TUDOR 1485-1603	STUART 1603-1714	GEORGIAN 1714-1837	VICTORIAN 1837-1901	MODERN TIMES 1902-NOW

How can I get hold of the Fire Brigade or hospital if they don't have a phone?!

On the Phone

Telephones came to Norwich in 1883. The new service cost £20 a year and had only 31 subscribers in the whole city. But you didn't need a phone then; the postal service was so fast you could write to somebody in the morning and have a reply by the afternoon. Thirty of the phones belonged to businesses and the only private line belonged to the house of Mr Jarrold. His telephone number was 26.

Power and Light

A gas works had been set up in 1825, next to the cathedral. This annoyed the Bishop as it was very ugly, smoky and smelly. By the 1880s, all the streets were lit by gas lamps and most people had gas light in their homes. In 1893 the Norwich Electricity set up a power station that provided electricity but very few homes used it. Most of the power went to factories and shops. For Queen Victoria's jubilee celebrations, the market place was lit with electric lights for the first time and everyone marvelled at how bright they were.

SPOT THIS!

This is the bandstand that replaced the iron one. It is still in use today.

Music in the Park

As Norwich's gardens were built over, the council made a new public park in Chapelfield Gardens in 1880. Brass band concerts were very popular and the council bought an extraordinary iron bandstand for the new park. It was made by a famous Norwich firm of ironfounders who specialised in making elaborate and complicated iron constructions. The bandstand wasn't popular with musicians as it was very draughty and it was scrapped in 1949.

How do we know?

The City Council has plans and drawings for many of the best-known buildings. Some of them can be seen at the Norfolk Record Office where they are kept safe.

An annual, called Kelly's Directory, gives lists and information on all the business and services in Norwich from 1831 to modern times.

The archives of the Norwich Mercury and Eastern Daily Press newspapers give lots of information about the openings of new buildings and businesses. Journalists then were often paid by the word so they tended to write a lot. What was probably a bit too much boring detail then is very useful to us historians now.

Time for Change

The streets are eerily silent after the day and night of drumming, thunderous rain and the surging roar of water cascading through the streets. The houses rise from the water reflected in a placid lake. The normal sound of horses' hooves and iron wheels clattering on the cobbles is changed to the creak and splash of oars, as boats carefully navigate streets that are now muddy rivers. It's rather like Venice but without the sun and romance.

A City of Slums

Norwich may have looked very quaint with its crowded courts of medieval buildings behind the new streets but the conditions that people lived in were shocking. Many had no water or sanitation and in some courts there were heaps of human dung nine feet high. In the 1920s, picturesque Elm Hill was a terrible slum and was only saved from being knocked down by the casting vote of the Mayor.

New flats were built in the city and big estates of houses with gardens were built on the outskirts. When the first of these council houses was finished, thousands of people came to see it. They couldn't believe that such a well-built, comfortable home could be rented for 80p a week.

SPOT THIS!

Have you walked down the medieval street of Elm Hill?

The Council realised something had to be done and began a programme of demolishing the old decaying houses.

The Great Flood

Norwich became famous in August 1912, when it was hit by the worst ever floods. It rained without stopping for 29 hours. 186.5 millimetres of rain fell. The drains choked, the river overflowed and nearly 4,000 houses were flooded. In some places the water was 3 metres deep. Three people died and thousands had to sleep in schools and church halls. People were trapped upstairs in their homes. Caley's chocolate factory rushed to help by sending out boats with milk and hot chocolate in bottles with a loop of string in the neck. These were passed up to the windows on the end of boat hooks.

This bronze lion, one of a pair, guards the steps to the City Hall. They were made by sculptor Robert Hardiman and are now the symbols of the city.

A workman still climbs 167 steps every three weeks to wind the clock.

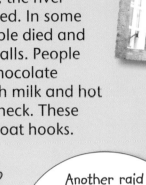

Another raid almost destroyed the cathedral but the firewatchers managed to put the fire bombs out.

War in Norwich

When war broke out in 1939, Norwich stayed untouched until 1942. On two nights in April, 1942, over 300 high explosives and thousands of fire bombs were dropped on the city. 254 people were killed, hundreds of houses and several churches destroyed and Caleys Chocolate factory burnt out. The next day the city smelled of soot and chocolate. Many people walked out of the city each night to sleep in the country.

How do we know?

There were many letters and articles in the Norwich newspapers about the state of the slums. The debates of the City Council were reported like this speech by Mabel Clarkson, the first woman to be elected. 'I know most of the Courts and Yards in Norwich, and I say that many of the dwellings in which families are living are a disgrace to this fine city. Those who want little children to grow up in healthy surroundings...those who want to stop all the sickness and suffering caused by bad housing must join me in working to get rid of the slums.'

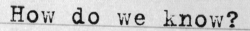

Norwich Today and Tomorrow...

Since 1300, Norwich has slipped down the chart of English cities from second to thirty-second place. It still has many historical buildings, great museums and a collection of books and records to tell us about the past. But what will we leave behind to tell our children and our children's children of what is still, as George Borrow called it, 'a fine city'?

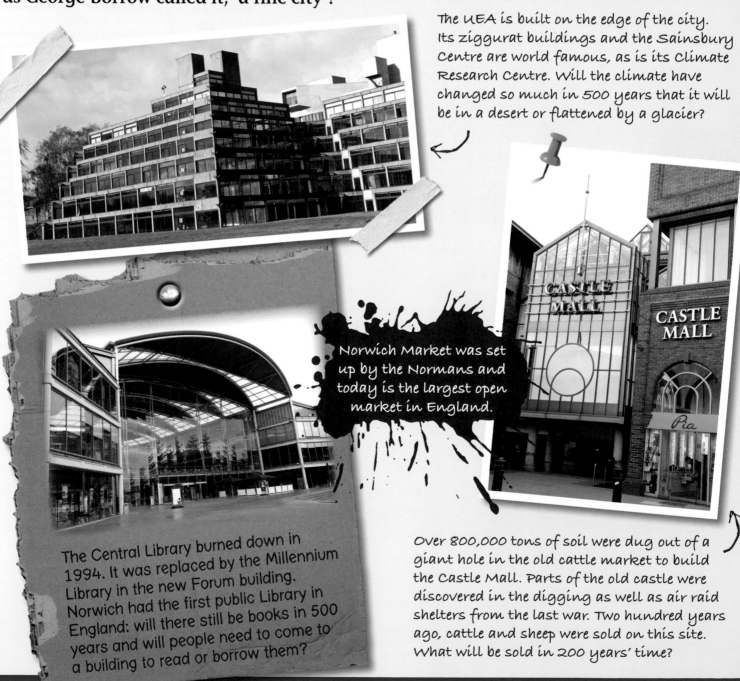

The UEA is built on the edge of the city. Its ziggurat buildings and the Sainsbury Centre are world famous, as is its Climate Research Centre. Will the climate have changed so much in 500 years that it will be in a desert or flattened by a glacier?

Norwich Market was set up by the Normans and today is the largest open market in England.

The Central Library burned down in 1994. It was replaced by the Millennium Library in the new Forum building. Norwich had the first public Library in England: will there still be books in 500 years and will people need to come to a building to read or borrow them?

Over 800,000 tons of soil were dug out of a giant hole in the old cattle market to build the Castle Mall. Parts of the old castle were discovered in the digging as well as air raid shelters from the last war. Two hundred years ago, cattle and sheep were sold on this site. What will be sold in 200 years' time?

The river which used to be full of barges and small cargo ships is now only used by pleasure cruisers. All the warehouses and factories have been replaced by flats and restaurants. Will it ever be used again to transport goods?

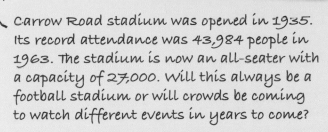

Carrow Road stadium was opened in 1935. Its record attendance was 43,984 people in 1963. The stadium is now an all-seater with a capacity of 27,000. Will this always be a football stadium or will crowds be coming to watch different events in years to come?

Norwich Market has been going for nearly 1,000 years. It's open every day except Sunday. Its 190 stalls sell just about everything you could ever need. Will it be there in another 1,000 years' time?

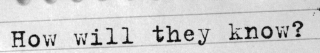

How will they know?

With today's ever-developing technology — and the possibility of more library fires! — historians of the future may have to rely more on emails, CDs, texts and even Facebook postings. Every time a new building is built in Norwich, archaeologists find more things that tell us about the history and growth of the city. What will we leave to be found under the buildings we construct?

It might be a small city but it's got more churches and museums than anywhere else.

Glossary

Abbey – a Christian monastery or convent, run by an Abbot.

AD – a short way of writing the Latin words anno Domini, which mean 'in the year of our Lord', i.e. after the birth of Christ.

Amphitheatre – a round, open-air theatre, surrounded by seats which rise from the centre so everyone can see.

Apprenticeship – the time served by a person learning a craft or trade.

Archaeologist – a person who studies the past by looking at the remains left by people in the past.

Barbarian – a savage person.

BC – a short way of writing 'before the birth of Christ'.

Catholic – a member of the Christian religion that considers the Pope to be the head of its church.

Effigy – an image of a person, often in the form of a sculpture.

Friary – a place where men of certain religious orders of the Roman Catholic Church lived.

Latin – a language originally spoken in Ancient Rome.

Leper – a person who has a disease called leprosy.

Medieval – a period of time roughly from the year 1000 to the 15th century.

Merchant – a person who buys and sells goods in order to make a living.

Mint – a place where coins are made.

Monastery – a place where monks live and worship.

Monk – a male member of a religious community that has rules of poverty, chastity and obedience.

Musket – a long-barrelled gun, loaded from the front, used from the 16th to the 18th centuries.

Musketeer – a soldier armed with a musket.

Nave – the central area of a church.

Norseman – another name for a Viking.

Parliamentarian – also known as a Roundhead.

Pike – a sharp spear on a long pole.

Plague – a serious disease that is carried by rats and can be transferred to humans by fleas.

Privy – a room or building with a toilet inside.

Roundhead – anyone who fought on the side of Parliament against Charles I in the English Civil War.

Royal Charter – written permission from the king or queen to do something.

Royalist – anyone who fought on the side of King Charles I in the English Civil War.

Undercroft – a cellar or storage room.

Workhouse – a place where poor people lived and worked when they had nowhere else to go.

Index

CELT
500 BC

ROMAN
AD 43–410

ANGLO-SAXON
AD 450–1066

VIKING
AD 865–1066

MEDIEVAL TIMES
1066–1485